THE BASIC GUIDE TO
HOW TO READ MUSIC

HELEN COOPER

A Perigee Book

For Nicholas

Perigee Books are published by The Putnam Publishing Group,
200 Madison Avenue, New York, NY 10016.

Copyright © 1982 by Omnibus Press. All rights reserved. This book, or parts thereof,
may not be reproduced in any form without permission.
Published simultaneously in Canada by General Publishing Co. Limited, Toronto.

Art direction: Robin Hardy   Designer: Lesley Bowman

Library of Congress Cataloging in Publication Data
Cooper, Helen. The basic guide to how to read music. "A Perigee Book"—t.p.
1. Music—Instruction and study.   2. Musical notation.   I. Title.
MT6.C7782H7   1982   781.6'33   84-19032   ISBN 0-399-51122-9

Printed in the United States of America
First Perigee Printing 1985
7   8   9   10

CONTENTS

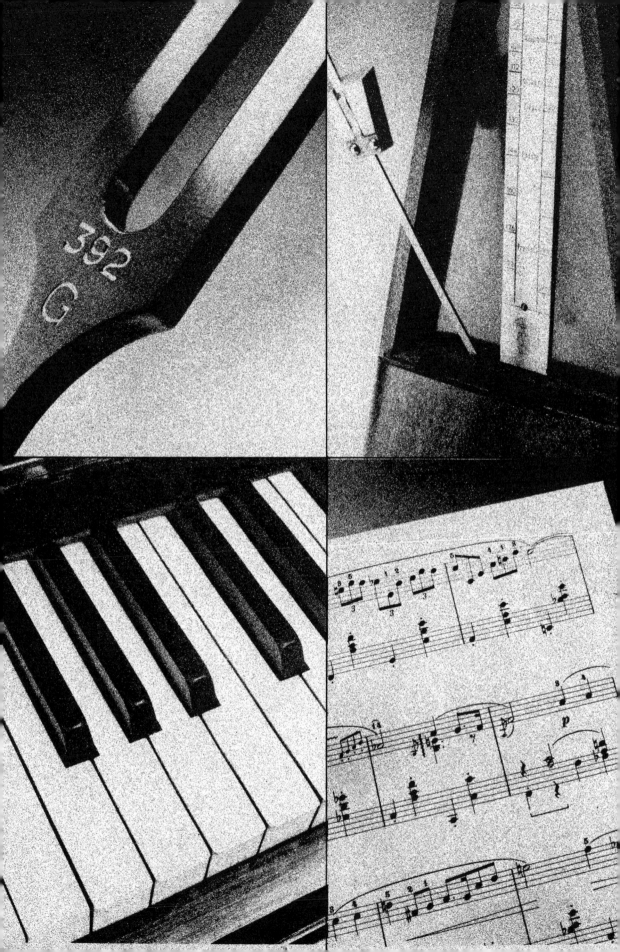

INTRODUCTION

How to Read Music is a clear and comprehensive guide for the instrumentalist who feels the need for a systematic introduction to the written language of music. Few teachers have sufficient time in an instrumental lesson to explain theoretical concepts in any depth and most students need such information in written form for easy reference.

This book is a guide for those whose interest in music has already been stimulated, but who still lack a solid foundation of basic technical knowledge. To be a competent instrumentalist, you need good co-ordination of ear, eye and touch. Your teacher will be concerned that your awareness and sensitivity develop with a reasonable degree of equality in all three senses. How to Read Music helps to make this process seem less daunting by giving your eye a clear image of what your ear can expect to hear.

It is difficult to appreciate the written language of music without translating it into sound. It is meaningless to study only the theoretical aspect without practical application. So it is vital that you perform and listen, in order to understand exactly what is contained within the structure of music.

Throughout musical history, composers have created a stunning array of tonal colours and an infinite variety of rhythm patterns from the same basic palette. When listening to music, you'll notice that the composer seeks to create contrasts. Different instruments can produce sounds of varying *timbre* and sonority, either in single threads or woven together in harmony or dissonance, sometimes interrupted by measured silence. All these elements are combined by a composer in order to create his individual style.

In Chapter 1, you'll find basic information concerning pitch and an explanation of what the word means in a specialized sense to a musician. Chapter 2 discusses the concept of rhythm. The easiest way to understand how pitch and rhythm can be organized into musical forms is to listen to as many different styles of music as possible.

Since most students have access to a keyboard, I've used a keyboard diagram as a visual explanation of the points in Chapter 3. It certainly makes the concepts of tones and semitones, sharps and flats considerably easier for you to understand, as it's the clearest visual image that can be related to the stave. Try to memorize that image in order to relate each note to your own instrument – and to the keyboard. That way, the ideas in Chapter 3 will fall into place.

The most effective way to become fluent in reading musical language is to study and sing melodies with which you are familiar. By singing the melody and following the shape of the printed notation, you will learn an enormous amount about the construction of music. You'll find various examples of this exercise throughout the book. The importance of the method cannot be overstated, and it will also help you to understand the structure of rhythms.

Not all symbols written above or below a musical score have a fixed or absolute meaning; some elements of musical language are open to interpretation. The degree of subtlety in a performance depends, to some extent, on an interesting and original reading of these elements. This is the vital fourth dimension in any performance. In the early stages, interpretation will be a matter for discussion with your teacher, who should encourage you to become more reliant upon your own judgement. As you gain experience, you will develop your own style and, through your growing technical skill, you'll find the means to express your unique musical personality.

It must be stressed that, although the concepts dealt with in this book still exist as a composer's most important building materials, forms and structures in music have undergone radical change in this century – just as they have in the visual arts. There are many excellent books which explain this change, and it is vital to understand how and why it has taken place. First, however, you must be able to read and comprehend conventional musical language and terms of reference.

Helen Cooper

Helen Cooper, London, 1982

The reader may find the following publications useful when studied in conjunction with this book:

Student Guide to Writing Music Notation by Glen Rosecrans (Wise Publications).

The Promenade Theory Papers by Poldi Zeitlen & David Goldberger (Yorktown Music Press).

I

PITCH

The Concept of Pitch

Pitch expresses the relative "height" or "depth" of a sound. Everyone is familiar with everyday sounds which have a high or low pitch: a blackbird's song is high pitched, and so is the sound of a high speed drill; the rumble of thunder is low pitched. Men tend to possess lower pitched speaking voices than women, and the voices of most people drop in pitch as they get older.

Musicians need a specialized language for expressing the concept of pitch. Scientists can quantify pitch by the measurement of the number of vibrations per second produced by a sound, but this knowledge written down would be too unwieldy for use by a musician. Symbols are needed to express pitch, and such symbols are known as **notes**.

In this first chapter, we will examine the most basic information provided by **notes** relating to **pitch**, but, before this information can be understood, it is necessary to examine the stage set – the environment in which musical notation is situated, because it provides the musician with the means to interpret vital information about each note.

The Staff

The **staff** provides the musician with a flexible visual system for perceiving and interpreting pitch. It consists of five equally spaced parallel lines which enclose four spaces.

A Staff

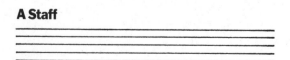

It is difficult for the eye to differentiate quickly and easily between more than five lines and four spaces. Keeping the staff comprehensible at a glance facilitates the fluent and accurate recognition of pitch, and the importance of the development of this skill should not be underestimated.

Many pieces of information are written on, above, and below the staff. They relate to many different elements concerned with the performance of the piece. The first important symbol to notice is the **clef** which is generally found at the beginning of each line of music.

The Clef

The staff is unable to provide any information about the pitch of a note unless it is qualified by a **clef**. There are four different clefs in common usage, but initially it is easier to understand the relationship between only three – the **treble**, the **alto** and the **bass** clefs. The fourth, the **tenor** clef, will be explained later in the chapter.

By placing a clef on the staff, a zone of pitch is established. The clefs form an integral and related system.

Treble Clef: Medium to high zone of pitch

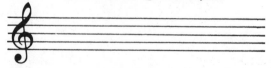

Alto Clef: Medium zone of pitch

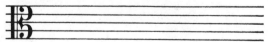

Bass Clef: Low to medium zone of pitch

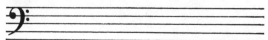

Music for most orchestral instruments is written on one staff only and uses just one clef – that which is appropriate to the zone of pitch for each specific instrument. The treble clef is used for the violin, flute, oboe, clarinet, horn and trumpet. The alto clef is used for the viola, and the bass clef for the 'cello, double bass, bassoon, bass trombone and tuba.

Piano music is written on two staffs which are bracketed together. The right hand usually plays higher pitched music written in the treble clef, while the left hand deals with lower pitched music written in the bass clef. After mastering the treble and bass clefs individually, a pianist must soon learn how to read these two clefs simultaneously.

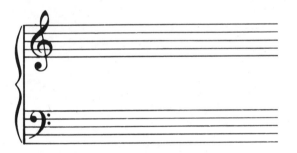

A staff qualified by a clef provides the correct environment for notes, which will now have a certain fixed pitch.

Notes

A **note** on a staff provides two fundamental pieces of information. First, it indicates a fixed pitch; second, it gives *some* information, though not all, as to the length of time it must last. This will be discussed in the second chapter. In this section, only the pitch function of notes will be examined. Notes may be written on a line or in a space between two lines.

on a line   in a space

The first seven letters of the alphabet are used to identify notes: **A,B,C,D,E,F, G.** This pattern indicates ascending pitch. These letter names are repeated to represent notes at a higher or lower pitch. Most orchestral instruments have the range to play each letter name at least twice, and it is important to identify precisely which note is required. Descending pitch is named in reverse order.

Notes in the Treble Clef:

Ascending   Descending

D E F G A B C D E F G   G F E D C B A G F E D

Notes in the Alto Clef:

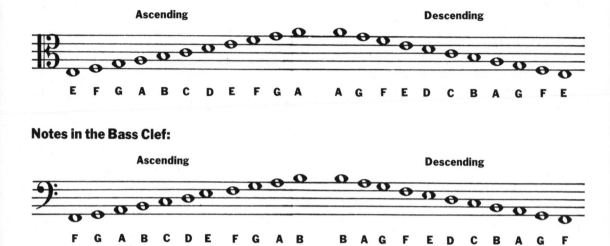

Notes in the Bass Clef:

Students who learn instruments using only one clef tend to become fluent in reading that one particular clef. Nevertheless, it is desirable to be able to read other clefs, and vital to understand the way in which the zones of pitch connect and overlap to form an integrated system.

In order to appreciate how this system functions, study the diagram below:

The extra line between the treble and bass clefs is called **middle C**. It is positioned below the treble staff, in the middle of the alto staff, and above the bass staff. This note is situated approximately in the centre of the piano keyboard. The alto clef overlaps with the lower zone of the treble clef and the upper zone of the bass clef.

It was once supposed that this "Great Staff" of eleven lines was used by composers centuries ago as a means of notating music. This idea is now generally discredited, and the "Great Staff" may be regarded only as a useful diagrammatic method of explanation of pitch zones and clef integration.

Leger Lines

The system of five lines and four spaces may be extended beyond the staff in order to avoid the necessity of changing clef. This system of extension is the same in all clefs. The extra lines added to the staff are called **leger lines**, and are only long enough to write one note upon, below or above. If you study the diagram below, you will notice this makes notation easier to read than the addition of solid continuous lines.

Treble Clef:

Alto Clef:

Bass Clef:

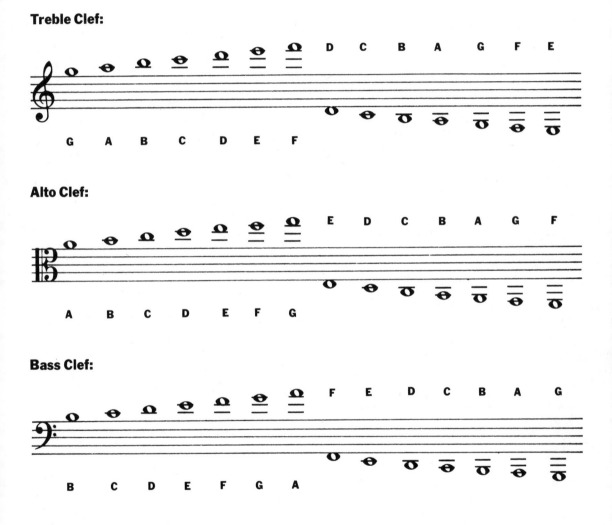

Other Clefs

Throughout the history of music, the alto clef symbol has been adapted to other zones of pitch, creating the **soprano** and **mezzo-soprano** clefs above the alto clef, and the **tenor** and **baritone** clefs below the alto clef.

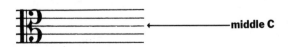

middle C

13

By moving this clef up and down the staff so that different lines are enclosed by the sign, it is possible to move middle C, thus changing the zone of pitch available on the stave.

Soprano   Mezzo-   Alto   Tenor   Baritone
          soprano

Of the above, only the tenor clef is now in common usage and indicates a zone of pitch between the alto and the bass clefs. It is used by the alto and tenor trombones, and for the higher registers of the bassoon and 'cello, where leger lines would be too numerous to be practical.

Naming Notes

Identify the clef on the staff, and then name the notes. When working on the clef appropriate to your instrument, try to work out how you would play each note.

Following the Shape of a Melody

Below is a French folk tune, "Ah dirais-je vous Maman" which has become well known as the nursery rhyme, "Twinkle, Twinkle, Little Star". First, identify the clef and name the notes; then, sing the tune following the shape of the melody.

As you were singing the tune you will have become aware that certain notes in it were of longer duration than others. The relationship between the duration of notes is another vital element in the performance of music. The next chapter seeks to explain the meaning of the concept of rhythm and the way in which it is notated.

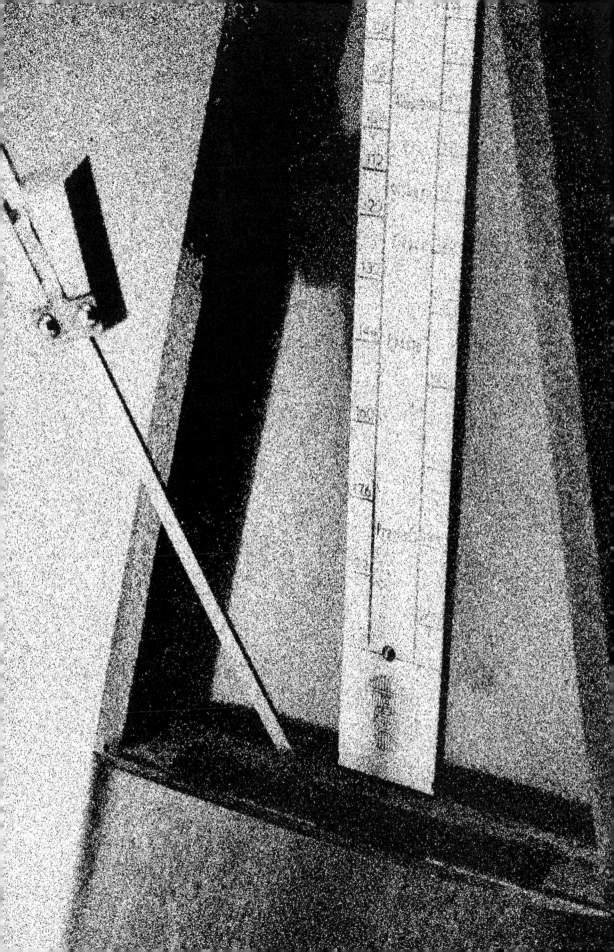

2
RHYTHM

The Concept of Rhythm

Rhythm is a concept that cannot be defined in a simple way. It is a term which can be used to express several related ideas which are all, in some way, concerned with the "time" element in music. The specific terms of reference are **pulse, stress** and **speed**. All these expressions will be explained later in this chapter.

In the previous chapter, the pitch function of a note was discussed. Each note has a second function, which is to express its duration, relative to the pulse of the music.

It must be stressed that pitch is a fixed and absolute system of values, while rhythm is a relative and flexible one, which cannot function without some degree of interpretation. It is vital to seek the guidance of your teacher when dealing with this aspect of your studies.

In order for you to understand the relationships between lengths of notes, it is necessary to explain the function of the pulse or beat in music. Pulse is the equal division of time. The easiest way to understand this concept is to listen to the ticking of a clock, or to feel the pulse in your own wrist.

In music, the pulse or beat provides the basic *structure* around which the *rhythm* of the music is built. The speed of the pulse will differ from piece to piece, and often varies within a piece, either at the direction of the composer or at the discretion of the performer. For the performer, there is also an element of interpretation as to where to place the various component parts of the beat, so that the music should not become relentless or mechanical. This is a very important factor in the creation of a subtle and sensitive performance.

Rhythm Values

Rhythm values fall into two categories – **simple** and **compound**. At this initial stage, it is only necessary to be able to comprehend the visual difference. Compound values are followed by a dot, and simple values are not.

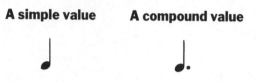

A simple value   A compound value

Simple Rhythm Values

It is important to understand the simple system fully, because the compound system is based upon it. Both have an equally important function in music notation. In the diagram below, you will see notated the six basic simple values in common usage, together with an explanation of their relative lengths.

a **whole note**
which sounds twice as long as

a **half note**
which sounds twice as long as

a **quarter note**
which sounds twice as long as

an **eighth note**
which sounds twice as long as

a **sixteenth note**
which sounds twice as long as

a **thirty-second note**

Here is another visual method of comprehending these relationships:

The previous diagram may be translated into the following ratios. Notice also the British names for simple rhythm values.

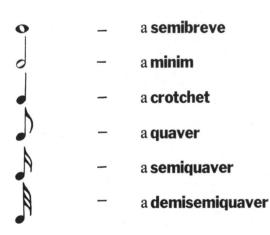

   —   a **semibreve**

   —   a **minim**

   —   a **crotchet**

   —   a **quaver**

   —   a **semiquaver**

   —   a **demisemiquaver**

All the diagrams in this section express the same set of ideas in different visual forms. Memorize the relationships between simple rhythm values. It will help you to understand compound rhythm values, and both simple and compound time signatures.

Compound Rhythm Values

Compound rhythm values are usually referred to as **dotted notes,** as they are followed by a dot. It is important to place the dot to the right of the note, not over or under, as this sign has a different meaning. A dot placed after a note adds exactly 50% more length to that note, so that it will sound half as long again. Thus, a compound value can be understood as 1½ times the length of the related simple value. A rhythm value of this type is most easily divisible by three, and has three component parts. It is useful to be able to break down a dotted note into its component parts at sight, as a unit of 1½ is rather unwieldy.

A half note may be viewed as a single unit without analyzing its components. But **a dotted** half note is easier to understand when broken down into the form of three quarter notes.

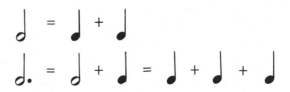

The same system applies to all other dotted notes. It is useful to practice identifying the simple components of compound values.

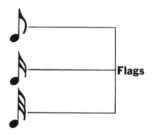

When your reading becomes more fluent, you will find that it is unnecessary to make a conscious effort to split a compound value into its component parts, and you'll be able to comprehend a compound value at a glance – just as when reading words it is unnecessary to break them down into constituent letters. It is now possible to understand how a rhythmic vocabulary is built up of values divisible by two or three, either simple or compound. Neither building brick is more common in music than the other, but it does perhaps require slightly more effort to learn to break down and re-combine the compound structures. This breaking down and subsequent reconstruction of component parts is a very important accomplishment for the musician who wishes to become an accurate and skilful sight reader.

Note Stems

All rhythm values, except whole notes, have vertical **stems**. Stems may be written pointing upwards or downwards.

The direction of the stem does not affect the pitch or length of the value in any way. Normally, to keep the music tidy and clear, notes above the middle line of the staff have stems which point downwards, and notes below the middle line have stems which point upwards. On the middle line they may point either way (depending on the notation of the rest of the bar).

Flags and Beams

The symbol at the end of the stem which gives separate identity to the eighth note, sixteenth note and thirty-second note, is known as a **"flag"**.

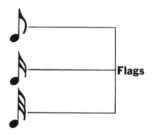

When multiples of flagged values occur together they may be joined by **"beams"**.

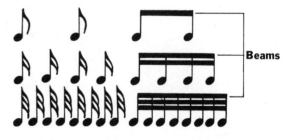

The use of beams in relation to the grouping of rhythm values will be discussed in more detail later in the chapter.

Rests

One of the most interesting aspects of rhythm in music is the relationship between sound and silence. The significance of silence as a positive contribution to music should not be underestimated. Great composers have always exploited the relationship between sound and silence to great effect. The notated symbols for silence are called **rests** and they measure precisely the all important silence between sounds. The pulse remains constant unless there are directions in the score to the contrary. A quarter rest may be expressed by two different symbols.

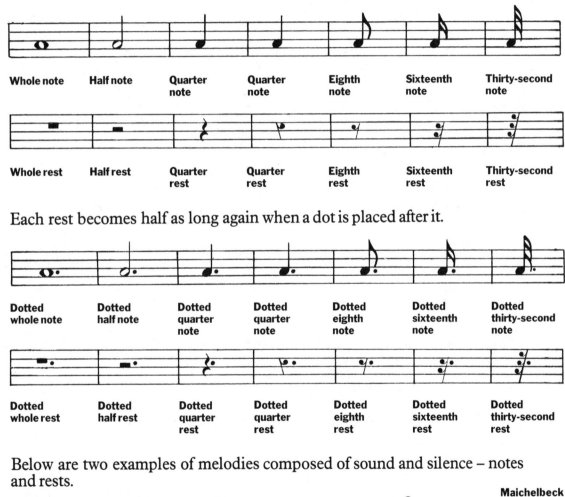

Whole note	Half note	Quarter note	Quarter note	Eighth note	Sixteenth note	Thirty-second note

Whole rest	Half rest	Quarter rest	Quarter rest	Eighth rest	Sixteenth rest	Thirty-second rest

Each rest becomes half as long again when a dot is placed after it.

Dotted whole note	Dotted half note	Dotted quarter note	Dotted quarter note	Dotted eighth note	Dotted sixteenth note	Dotted thirty-second note

Dotted whole rest	Dotted half rest	Dotted quarter rest	Dotted quarter rest	Dotted eighth rest	Dotted sixteenth rest	Dotted thirty-second rest

Below are two examples of melodies composed of sound and silence – notes and rests.

Maichelbeck

Schumann

Bars (Measures) and Barlines

Barlines divide music into sections called **bars (or measures),** which contain an equal number of pulses or beats. The number and nature of the beats in each bar (measure) will differ from piece to piece, and the appropriate information will be found in the time signature. The end of a piece, or the end of a section within it, will be marked by two adjacent vertical lines. This device is called a **double barline.**

Rosamunde theme

barline

bar (measure)

Schubert

double barline

My Country 'Tis of Thee

barline

bar (measure)

double barline

Stresses in Music

Within the framework of each bar (measure), certain pulses will be stronger than others. Conventionally, the first beat of the bar (measure) will have the strongest pulse and subsequent beats will be weaker. Composers have created brilliant effects by destroying this convention and thus undermining the listener's sense of pulse. At this stage, it is necessary only to be able to identify the degree of importance conventionally accorded to each beat of the bar (measure) – seek your teacher's help with this.

Time Signatures

The composer may utilize any rhythm value as the beat, but it is most usual to use the half note, quarter note or eighth note. Sixteenth notes are sometimes used, but less commonly.

As you now know, music has a natural pulse, and barlines mark the natural divisions created by the stresses in the music. Obviously, it is useful to know which way the pulse is grouped before acquainting yourself with the pitch and rhythm patterns of the piece. So, we need two pieces of information: we need to know how many beats in the bar (measure), and also whether those beats are half notes, quarter notes or eighth notes.

The symbol which gives us this information is found at the beginning of the first line of the music, after the clef and the key signature. It is a symbol consisting of two numbers and it is called the **time signature**. The two numbers that make up the time signature provide the musician with two different pieces of information. The top number signifies how many beats in each bar (measure), and the bottom number is a "code" which shows which type of rhythm value is being used – i.e. half note, quarter note, eighth note or sixteenth note.

The code for this is as follows:

2 half notes

4 quarter notes

8 eighth notes

16 sixteenth notes

Now refer back to the previous section concerning simple rhythm values. The above code is derived from the ratios between lengths of values. Here are some examples of time signatures and an explanation of their meaning:

$\dfrac{4}{8} = 4$ eighth note beats in a bar (measure)

$\dfrac{3}{4} = 3$ quarter note beats in a bar (measure)

$\dfrac{2}{2} = 2$ half note beats in a bar (measure)

Time signatures are categorized in two ways: **simple** and **compound**. These classifications relate to simple and compound rhythm values.

Simple Time Signatures

The following time signatures may be classified as simple:

$$\frac{2}{8} \quad \frac{3}{8} \quad \frac{4}{8} \mid \frac{2}{4} \quad \frac{3}{4} \quad \frac{4}{4} \mid \frac{2}{2} \quad \frac{3}{2} \quad \frac{4}{2}$$

Sometimes the time signature $\frac{4}{4}$ is notated as a capital letter **C**. Similarly the time signature $\frac{2}{2}$ may appear as **₵**.

The following characteristics of **simple time signatures** should be observed: the top number is *not* a multiple of three – this is the visual distinction between simple and compound time signatures. In compound time signatures the top number *is* a multiple of three and the significance of this will be explained in the next section. Simple time signatures give straightforward information about the type of beat and the number of beats in each bar (measure).

Look at these examples:

2 quarter beats in each bar (measure) — Kuhlau

3 eighth beats in each bar (measure) — Nichelmann

3 half note beats in each bar (measure) — Byrd

2 half note beats in each bar (measure) — Purcell

Compound Time Signatures

In a **compound time signature**, the top number *is* a multiple of three, and this is a significant factor in the interpretation of the time signature. The following are the most common compound time signatures:

6 9 12 | 6 9 12 | 6 9 12
16 16 16 | 8 8 8 | 4 4 4

The two numbers comprising the compound time signature are translated in the same way as for a simple time signature. The top number indicates the number of beats in each bar (measure), and the bottom number is a code for the type of beat. In the examples above,

16 = a sixteenth

8 = an eighth

4 = a quarter

There is, in the compound time signature, another element to be considered. Refer back to the section of this chapter which explains compound rhythm values. When beats are brought together in groups of three, another unit is formed–a compound rhythm value, or dotted note. This unit is sometimes considered to be the pulse. For example, in $\frac{6}{8}$ there are two dotted quarter pulses; in $\frac{12}{8}$ there are four dotted quarter pulses; in $\frac{6}{4}$ there are three dotted half pulses; and in $\frac{12}{16}$ there are four dotted eighth pulses.

This information is tabulated below.

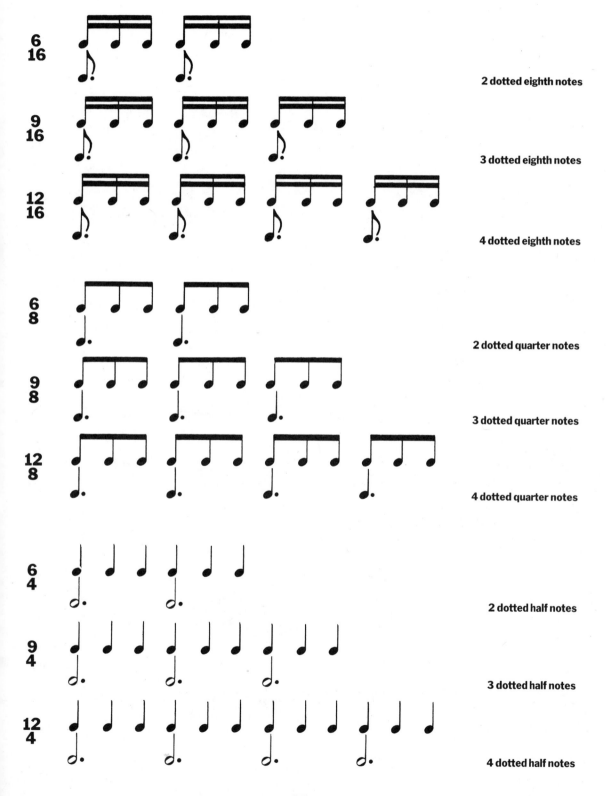

Read through the following examples. Try to identify where the dotted quarter pulse will occur in the first group, and the dotted eighth pulse in the second group.

Group 1

6 eighths in each bar (measure) — Gruber

6 eighths in each bar (measure) — Attrib. Henry VIII

9 eighths in each bar (measure) — Telemann

12 eighths in each bar (measure) — Handel

12 eighths in each bar (measure) — Bach

Group 2

12 sixteenths in each bar (measure) — Hummel

9 sixteenths in each bar (measure) — Bach

The main *difference* between simple and compound time signatures may be summed up thus: in a simple time signature, the bottom number gives clear information about the type of beat, and that beat generally does not need interpretation. In a compound time signature, the top number will be a multiple of three, showing that the beat may be as shown in the bottom number, *or* that it may be grouped in threes to form a dotted unit.

Time signatures may also be tabulated in the following way:

Simple Duple

All simple time signatures with two beats in a bar (measure) are called **simple duple.**

Simple Triple

All simple time signatures with three beats in a bar (measure) are called **simple triple.**

Simple Quadruple

All simple time signatures with four beats in a bar (measure) are called **simple quadruple.**

The system for naming compound time signatures takes into account the number of compound (dotted) beats in the bar (measure).

Compound Duple

All compound time signatures with two compound beats in a bar (measure) are called **compound duple**.

Compound Triple

All compound time signatures with three compound beats in a bar (measure) are called **compound triple**.

Compound Quadruple

All compound time signatures with four compound beats in a bar (measure) are called **compound quadruple**.

The Division and Reconstruction of the Beat

The time signature shows us how many beats there are in the bar (measure), and also the nature of those beats. As you know, the breaking down and subsequent reconstruction of the beat will be different in simple time and compound time.

In simple time, each beat may be broken down into rhythm values, which are worth one half, one quarter, one eighth, etc. of the beat. Groups of flagged rhythm values should be beamed together in such a way that the structure of the pulse is made clear.

If the time signature is $\frac{2}{2}$ (¢), then the half note beat may be broken down into any of its component parts:

1 half note

2 quarter notes

4 eighth notes

8 sixteenth notes

16 thirty-second notes

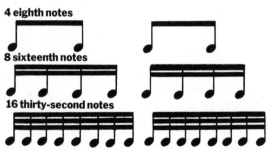

In addition, any of the above values may be combined to create interest in the rhythm:

Compound rhythm values (dotted notes), may also be used in simple time. Add up each pattern and you will see that in this instance the total always equals a half note:

Sometimes values are used which last longer than one beat. For example – in ¾ it is usual to find dotted quarters, half-notes and dotted half-notes, all of which are longer than the quarter beat:

There are many, many more rhythmic permutations occurring in simple time, as you will see in the examples at the end of this section.

In compound time, each dotted beat may be broken down into values which are worth one third, one sixth, one twelfth, etc. of the beat.

For example – in ⁹⁄₈ the dotted quarter beat may be broken down into any of its component parts:

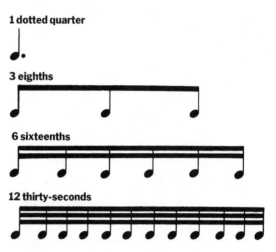

1 dotted quarter

3 eighths

6 sixteenths

12 thirty-seconds

In addition, any of the above values may be combined in mixed patterns:

Obviously, simple rhythm values (notes without a dot) may also be used in compound time, as the components of the dotted beat are simple values.

Compound values are used in compound time to create other permutations within the dotted pulse:

The Organization of Rhythm Values

When grouping rhythm values, the structure of the time signature must be made apparent. That is to say, a bar of $\frac{3}{2}$ must clearly show the three half-note beats. Likewise, a bar of $\frac{6}{4}$ must clearly show two dotted half-note beats. Notice that, in compound time, the dotted beat dictates the structure of the bar. Thus, beamed groups of rhythm values should demonstrate the structure of the pulse within the framework of the bar.

Look at the following examples:

Tunes in simple time

Brahms

Notice that the groups of eighth notes and sixteenth notes are never beamed across the beat but *are* beamed within it.

$\frac{3}{8}$ is an exception. Rhythm values are beamed in compound groups:

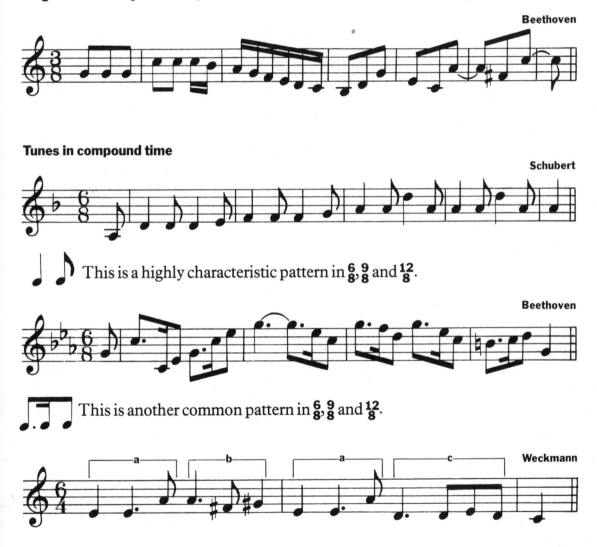

Beethoven

Tunes in compound time

Schubert

This is a highly characteristic pattern in $\frac{6}{8}$, $\frac{9}{8}$ and $\frac{12}{8}$.

Beethoven

This is another common pattern in $\frac{6}{8}$, $\frac{9}{8}$ and $\frac{12}{8}$.

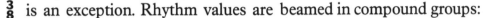

Weckmann

In $\frac{6}{4}$, there are two dotted half note beats in each bar (measure). In the tune above, you will see three different subdivisions of the dotted half note: a, b and c.

To sum up: The grouping of rhythm values is governed by one basic principle – that the rhythm, in the context of the beat, is made as clear as possible to the musician.

Learning to Read Rhythm Patterns

In the first instance, the best way to learn to read rhythm patterns is by observing written rhythmic notation of known melodies. With practice and guidance from your teacher, it will become possible to read and play com-pletely unfamiliar rhythms, and it is necessary to have acquired some skill in this in order to be able to sight read.

Look at the traditional tunes below: sing them through, follow the rhythm pattern and try to sense the pulse.

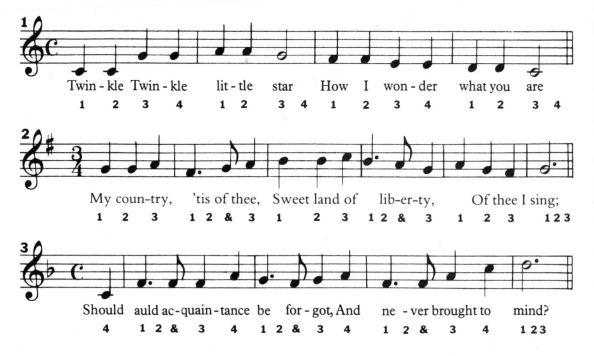

Let's look at the first example. Sing this through again, tapping out a regular beat at a moderate speed before you begin. Then sing it again, singing the *numbers* that identify the beats, instead of the words. This will show you how to count one beat on each quarter note and two beats on each half note.

Now look at the second and third melodies. Here you will learn how to assess the length of a dotted quarter note within the framework of a quarter pulse. Sing each melody through, tapping a regular quarter pulse. You will notice that in certain bars (measures) of each melody, the eighth note lies exactly half way between the second and third beats of the bar (measure). Practice both melodies, singing the numbers that identify the beats instead of the words.

The melodies we have dealt with so far have all been in simple time; now sing through the melodies below, both of which are in compound time.

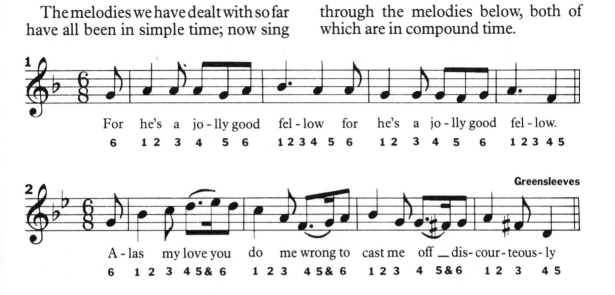

Look at the first example. Because this tune is in a fairly brisk style, the tempo will be quite fast; therefore, the beat will be a dotted quarter. But first of all, let's slow the pace of the music and split each bar (measure) into six eighth beats so as to understand the structure of the rhythm. Sing it through more slowly, tapping out six eighth beats in each bar. See how a quarter note lasts two eighth beats, and a dotted quarter note three eighth beats. Now sing it faster, tapping only the first and fourth eighth beats – i.e. the dotted quarter pulse. Here we have established an important rule: if the rhythm patterns are complex or confusing, break them down into the smallest component parts in order to understand the structure of the larger values.

Now look at the second melody. This is more thoughtful and languid, so could easily be counted in six. Tap out six eighth beats while singing this melody through again. Listen carefully to the dotted eighth/sixteenth/eighth pattern. This is a highly characteristic unit in compound time. When looking for the smallest component part, split the second eighth beat of the bar (measure) into two sixteenths.

Tied Notes

A **tie** is a curved line which links two notes of the same pitch. This device has four common uses. In all cases, the first note *only* is sounded, but it is held for its own length plus that of the note to which it is tied.

First, a tie may be used to indicate a continuous sound over a barline:

The last note of the first bar (measure) will sound for two quarter beats, but it obviously could not be written as a half note as this would create five quarter beats in the first bar (measure). Thus, the second beat of this note is notated in the next bar (measure) and the two symbols are joined by a tie sign:

Walther

Here two melodic lines are written on the same staff. This will happen often in keyboard music. The lower line could have been written as but the tied notation reveals the rhythm more clearly.

Second, a tie may be used instead of a dot where it is necessary for the musician to be able to see the component parts of a dotted value notated clearly. This could happen where two or more melodic lines sound together, as in this example above by Walther:

Third, a tie is used when a rhythm value written as one symbol would break the laws of good notational organization.

Look at the example below:

Beethoven

The first tie in the first bar enables the musician to see at a glance that the music is in $\frac{6}{8}$ and that the basic rhythmic structure of the bar comprises two dotted quarter notes. If the note had been written as a quarter note instead of two tied eighth notes, it would be easy to mistakenly interpret the passage in $\frac{3}{4}$:

Clearly $\frac{6}{8}$ and $\frac{3}{4}$ are *not* interchangeable, as the pulse of each has a different structure.

Fourth, a tie is used when a rhythm value cannot be expressed any other way – because there is no single symbol to represent its length:

Syncopation

Syncopation is the name given to cross rhythms which occur when notes that would normally be weak are given strong accents. This idea is best understood by looking carefully at the example below. At the places marked, the stress in the melody precedes the beat by one sixteenth.

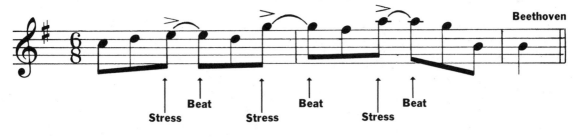

In the next example, the stress of the music occurs on the third and sixth eighths of the bar, one eighth before the natural stress on the first and fourth eighths.

Triplets and Duplets

Triplets

Sometimes a composer will need a notational device for dividing a simple rhythm value into three equal parts, and a compound rhythm value into two equal parts. In the example below you will see a bar of $\frac{3}{4}$ rhythm. $\frac{3}{4}$ is a simple time signature.

If the composer wishes to divide the second beat of the bar into three equal parts instead of two, it would be notated thus:

Note the small figure 3, which appears underneath the rhythm values. This indicates that three eighth notes will fill up the time normally occupied by two eighth notes – this is called a **triplet.** Below is a passage from the 1st movement of a Beethoven piano sonata, which vividly demonstrates the notation of triplets in the environment of a simple time signature. Note the time signature $\mathbb{C} = \frac{2}{2}$.

Duplets

In the following example, you will see a bar of $\frac{6}{8}$ rhythm. $\frac{6}{8}$ is a compound time signature.

Below you will see how the composer may replace the unit of three eighth notes with two eighth notes. This is called a **duplet:**

Note the small figure 2, indicating a duplet in compound time. The following example shows a duplet used in a compound time signature:

The eighth note is the rhythm value used in both examples, but the same rules apply to *all* other rhythm values – i.e., in $\frac{3}{2}$ there may be three quarter notes in the time of two quarter notes,

and in $\frac{9}{16}$ there may be two sixteenth notes in the time of three sixteenth notes:

There are many theoretical aspects of rhythm which have not been discussed, but all rhythmic complexities are built upon these basic principles.

3

THE FORMAL ORGANIZATION OF PITCH: THE STRUCTURE AND NOTATION OF INTERVALS, SCALES AND KEYS.

Section A

The Piano Keyboard

From the previous chapters, you will have gained some knowledge of the basic building materials of music – i.e., the notation and measurement of the more common symbols expressing pitch and rhythm. The next stage is to examine how pitch can be organized into structures: consecutive sounds form **melody**, and simultaneous sounds **harmony**. In this chapter you will learn something of the different ways that sound may be formally arranged, though the emphasis will be placed mainly on melodic, rather than harmonic, structures. The study of harmony as an academic discipline is more appropriate at a more advanced level, and there is no shortage of good material available for private or supervised study.

Intervals

The sonic distance between two different notes is called an **interval**. The method of naming different intervals will be discussed later in this chapter in sections B, C, and D. Accurate visual and aural recognition of intervals is an important skill for all musicians, aural recognition being particularly vital for singers and string players. The piano keyboard provides a clear link between the visual and aural aspects of intervals, and it is recommended that all students gain access to a keyboard and develop some fluency in the use of it.

The Octave

From the study of Chapter 1, you will have realized that if you begin counting from any one of the letter names used for naming notes, and pass up or down through eight note names, you will reach the same letter name as the one with which you began.

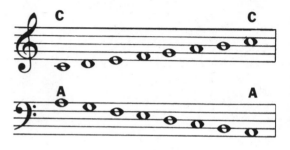

This interval – for example, C - C or A - A – comprises eight notes and is called an **octave** (from the Latin root meaning "eight") and is of fundamental importance in music. The octave unites two sounds so closely related that they have the same letter name.

Refer now to the diagram of the piano keyboard below.

Find middle C on the piano and then the note C which is one octave above. Play this octave sounding the lower note before the upper. Listen for the *similarity*, and then for the *difference* between the two notes. All possible tonal relations can be projected within an octave, and any system projected into an octave constitutes a scale.

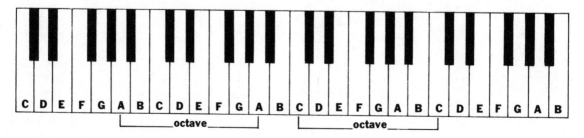

The Piano Keyboard

The piano keyboard usually contains seven or eight octaves, depending on the size and type of instrument. The diagrams in this section show only a small part of a typical keyboard.

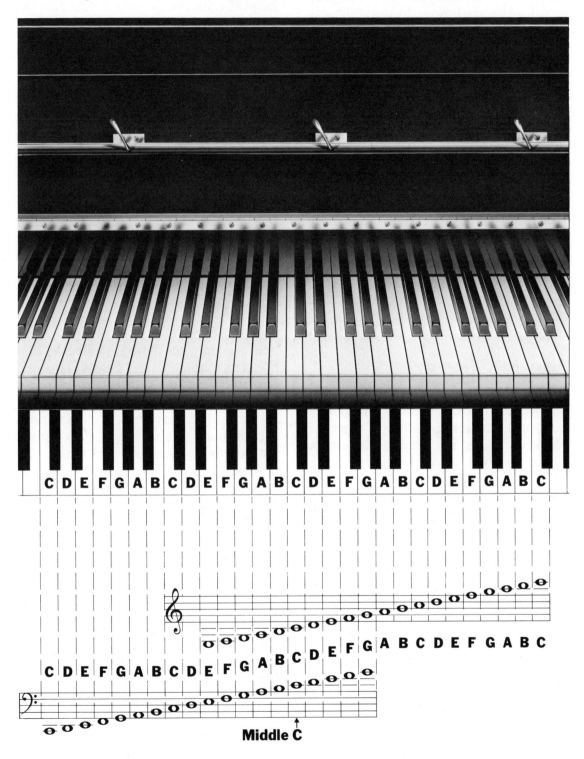

Middle C

The notes you have learned about in Chapter 1 are the white notes on the keyboard. The sequence of white and black notes has been designed in a way that enables the performer to find his way around the keyboard with the minimum of difficulty. It is important to familiarize yourself with this irregular arrangement of white and black notes as soon as possible. Look at the diagram (p.41). Reading upwards from middle C, you will notice that black notes occur in blocks of two and three. Notice also that some white notes have a black note between them, and some do not. If you look at the letter names on the keyboard, you will observe there is a black note between each of the following pairs of white notes:

C-D D-E F-G G-A A-B

There is no black note between these remaining pairs of white notes:

B-C E-F

Steps and Half steps

The entire keyboard is composed of **half steps.** Thus, the interval from any note to its nearest neighbour, whether black or white, is called a **half step.** There are two places in each octave where two adjacent white notes form a half step because there is no black note between them:

B-C E-F

Sharps, Flats and Naturals

It is necessary to have some understanding of sharps and flats in order to be able to name the black notes on the keyboard and to give a second name to some of the white notes.

Each black note has two letter names in common usage. (A third and fourth more obscure name for each note will be described later in this chapter). To find the first of these two names for a black note, refer to the white note a half step *below* it. With the addition of a **sharp** sign (♯) to its letter name, we have now created the correct symbol for naming this black note. To seek the other common name for each black note, refer to the white note a half step *above* it. To this letter name, add a **flat** sign (♭). The **natural** sign (♮) cancels the effect of a sharp (♯) or flat (♭) sign.

Thus, the black note above A and below B may be named A♯ or B♭. The black note above C and below D may be named C♯ or D♭. This rule for naming black notes also applies to B, C, E and F. As we have already seen, these notes are exceptional in some ways. The note B may in some circumstances be named C♭, as it is a half step below C, and C may be named B♯, as it is a half step above B. Similarly, the note E may be named F♭ and F named E♯.

The composer has a very limited choice in this matter, as the notation of each note will be arrived at by adherence to strict rules. At this stage, it is enough to understand that each sound may be

Sounds expressed by more than one written symbol

A♯ B♭ C♯ D♭ D♯ E♭ B♯ C♮ B♮ C♭ E♮ F♭ E♯ F♮

expressed by more than one written symbol, and it is not necessary to understand how to make that choice (p.42).

A **step** consists of two half steps. If you study the keyboard diagram, you will observe that C - C♯ and C♯ - D are both half steps. Thus, C-D is a step. G♯ -A and A-A♯ are both half steps, so G♯ -A♯ must be a step. Work through these examples at the piano, identifying the two half steps that comprise each step.

F - G   D - E   B - C♯   A♭ - B♭   E♭ - F

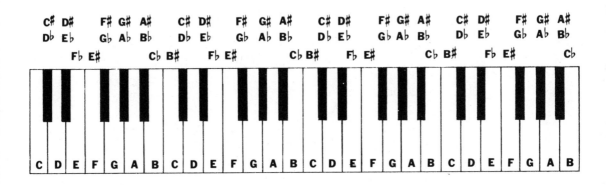

The correct choice of name for the upper note of a step is that which contains the next letter of the alphabet. It is important not to miss out a letter. Follow the first example through and you will see how it is possible to avoid making this error.

Example 1

Name the note which is one step above F♯.

If you look at the keyboard, you will see that the note one step above F♯ can be discovered by following through two half steps: F♯ - G, G - G♯. The note G♯ has two names: G♯ and A♭ but the correct name in this instance must be G♯ in order to satisfy the rule of consecutive lettering.

Example 2

Name the note which is one step above B♭.

Follow through the rule for finding the step by passing through two half steps

B♭ - B, B - C. Thus, a step above B♭ is C and this fulfils the rule of using two consecutive letter names.

Practice this skill at the piano until you can fluently name given half steps and steps without conscious effort. For string players, the understanding of half steps and steps is fundamental when seeking the precise position of any two consecutive notes on the fingerboard. Half steps are the building bricks of intervals, so fluency in the skill of identifying steps and half steps with ear and eye is *vital* for all musicians.

Now apply this knowledge to the instrument you are studying. If it is a stringed instrument, you will notice that there is a systematic method for seeking the distances between notes. In order to accomplish this task with accuracy, it is necessary to understand the precise distance between the two notes of the interval.

You now have enough knowledge to understand the construction of scales.

Section B

The Structure of the Major Scale

A **scale** is a set of notes either consistently rising or falling contained within an octave. The sequence of intervals within the scale must conform to one of several fixed forms. The most common forms – the **major** and **minor** – contain eight notes at irregular intervals, all of which have consecutive letter names. Major and minor scales provide the material for melody and harmony. A piece of music based on the notes contained in the scale of C major would be said to be in the key of C major.

The major scale has a fixed form. In order to study the intervals contained within it, let's examine the only major scale which may be played entirely on the white notes of the piano. Try this exercise at the keyboard. Find middle C and then play eight consecutive notes in ascending order which will bring you to the note C one octave above middle C. These are the notes you should have played:

C - D - E - F - G - A - B - C

Play this sequence again and listen carefully to the sounds you are creating. Play the notes in reverse order. Probably, these sounds are already familiar to your ear. Look at that one octave on the keyboard and work out the pattern of steps and half steps, and then study the diagram below to check whether you were correct. Note also that conventionally, the degrees of the scale are distinguished by Roman numerals.

C major has no sharpened or flattened notes. The sequence of intervals in this scale of **C major**, and in *all* other *major* scales, is as follows:

Step, step, half step, step, step, step, half step.

Try to commit this sequence to memory. Study also this same scale notated in the bass clef, beginning one octave lower. If you are studying an instrument for which music is written in the treble clef, try to become familiar with the bass clef as soon as possible.

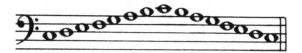

I II III IV V VI VIIVIIIVII VI V IV III II I

The Construction of Subsequent Sharp Major Scales.

When building major scales on other key notes, it is necessary to sharpen or flatten certain degrees of the scale in order to maintain the correct sequence of steps and half steps. This section describes only the scales which need to be modified by sharps.

However, before looking at examples of other major scales, we will examine the device known as a **tetrachord**. The scale of C major may be split into two halves, each of which is known as a tetrachord. In the major scale, the two tetrachords consist of identical intervals (two steps and a half step), and the interval between the two tetrachords is a step.

I II III IV V VI VII VIII VII VI V IV III II I

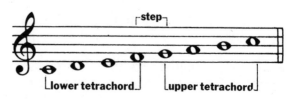

step

lower tetrachord   upper tetrachord

The diagram below provides the means to construct the major scale with one sharp. This scale begins on the fifth degree of C major (G), and utilizes the *upper* tetrachord of this key to form its own *lower* tetrachord. Four more consecutive notes must be added to create the upper tetrachord. In order to make a half step between the seventh and eighth degrees of the scale, it is necessary to raise the seventh degree by a half step. Thus, we have created the scale of G major, which has one sharp - F♯.

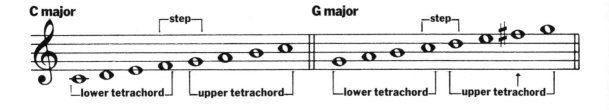

The major scale with two sharps (D), can be constructed in the same way. The upper tetrachord of G major becomes the lower tetrachord of D major. When the new upper tetrachord is added to this, the seventh degree must again be raised by a half step from C to C♯. Notice that D major possesses two sharps – F♯ and C♯.

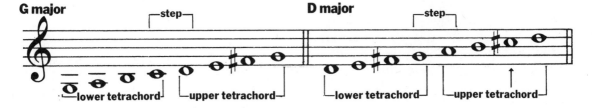

It is useful, at this point, to summarize the rules that have so far been established:

First, each subsequent sharp major scale begins on the *fifth* degree of the previous scale.

Second, each scale will retain the sharps from the previous scale and to those will be added the sharp that precedes the seventh degree of the scale.

Third, the sharps occur at the interval of a fifth.

In the following diagrams are all the major scales that contain sharps placed in relation to C major. Check the pattern of steps and half steps in each scale. (The half steps are marked with a bracket.)

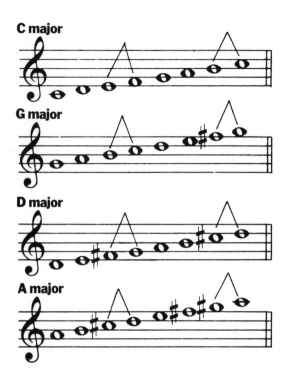

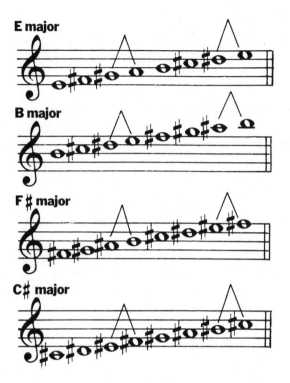

Flat Major Scales

Refer back to the scale of C major. This will also be our starting point for the creation of subsequent major scales which need modifying by flats. The tetrachord device, used in a slightly different way, again gives us a simple method of tracing the sequence of flat keys.

The key with one flat is F major. To create this scale take the *lower* tetrachord of C major as the *upper* tetrachord of the

new scale, and create a new lower tetrachord with the four preceding consecutive letter names. The degrees of the scale will now read:

F - G - A - B - C - D - E - F

If you play this pattern on the piano, you will notice that one note must be modified in order to create the correct step-half step pattern. B must be lowered by a half step to B♭ in order that the third and fourth degrees of the scale form an interval of a half step.

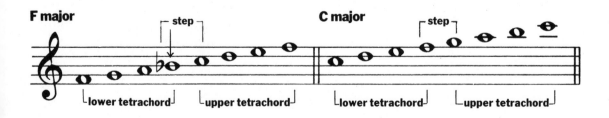

It is possible to notate the major scale that possesses two flats, B♭ major, by the application of the same process. The lower tetrachord of F major becomes the upper tetrachord of B♭ major. Four notes are placed before it, and the fourth of these is lowered by a half step from E to E♭. The first note will be B♭ because this is already established in the upper tetrachord.

B♭ major **F major**

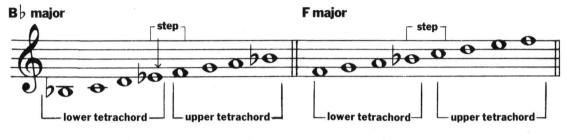

Below is a summary of the rules that apply to major scales modified by flats.

First, each subsequent flat major scale begins on the *fourth* degree of the previous scale.

Second, each scale will retain the flats from the previous scale, and to those will be added the flat that precedes the fourth degree of the scale.

Third, the flats occur at the interval of a fourth.

In the diagram below are all the major scales that contain flats placed in relation to C major. Check the pattern of steps and half steps in each scale. (The half steps are marked with a bracket.)

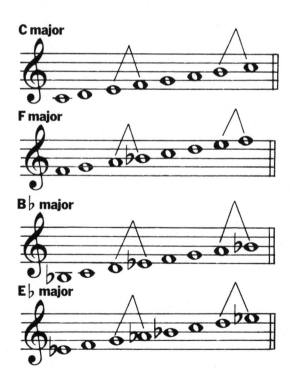

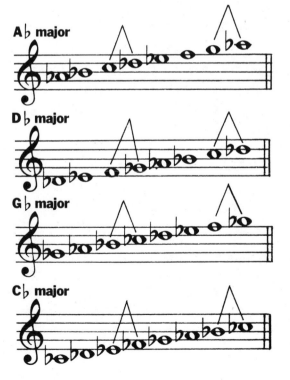

Technical Names for the Degrees of the Scale

In the diagram below you will see the technical note names applied to the scale of C major.

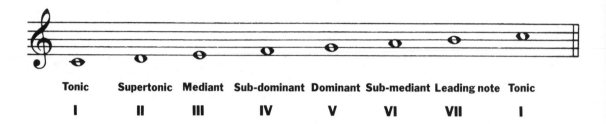

Tonic	Supertonic	Mediant	Sub-dominant	Dominant	Sub-mediant	Leading note	Tonic
I	II	III	IV	V	VI	VII	I

I **Tonic** This is the key note. It gives the scale its name.

II **Supertonic** This is the note immediately above the tonic.

III **Mediant** This note lies halfway between the tonic and the dominant.

IV **Sub-dominant** This is the note immediately below the dominant.

V **Dominant** This note is second in importance only to the tonic.

VI **Sub-mediant** This note lies half way between the (upper) tonic and the sub-dominant.

VII **Leading note** This note leads up to the (upper) tonic.

Intervals of the Major Scale

As you know, an interval is the measurement of the tonal space between two notes. In order to become fluent in naming any given interval, it is best to first learn how to identify the intervals between C and every other note in the major scale of C. This introduces the student to the simplest intervals in music.

There are two pieces of information contained in the name of each interval. As you will see from the diagram (p.49), the number refers to the inclusive number of letter names contained by the interval. The adjective before the number – i.e. **major** or **perfect** – provides precise information about the number of half steps within the interval. It is not necessary to understand how this system works at this stage: it is enough to memorize the names of the intervals, what they look like in C major and also, if you choose, to learn how many half steps are contained within each one. You can check this at the piano keyboard.

The most vital exercise is to *listen* to these intervals, playing the lower note first, followed by the upper, and then sounding the two notes together. Repeat this process vocally: play the lower note on the piano, then sing it; then play the upper note, and sing that. Then without the aid of the piano, sing first the lower and then the upper note again. Last, play the two notes together and then sing the lower and the upper note, separating the sounds in your mind.

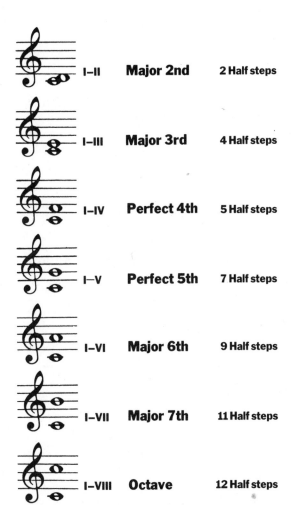

When learning to recognize intervals, it is useful to make associations between well known melodies and the intervals you are trying to grasp. For example, the interval between the first two notes of "Auld Lang Syne" is a perfect 4th. The interval between the second and third notes of "Twinkle, Twinkle Little Star" is a perfect 5th, while that between the first and second notes of "My Bonnie Lies Over The Ocean" is a major 6th. The interval between the first two notes of "While Shepherds Watched" is a major 3rd, and that between the second and third notes of "My Country 'Tis of Thee" is a major 2nd. By linking these intervals to melodies that you already know, you are helping yourself to under-stand them as quickly and as easily as possible.

Key Signatures

You will remember that compositions based on a given scale will be said to be in the key of that name. Music would be very difficult to read if there was a sharp or flat written in front of every note that required one. For this reason, the sharps or flats required for a given key – the **key signature** – are notated in a standard pattern at the beginning of each line of music.

The sharps are always written in the following order:

F♯ C♯ G♯ D♯ A♯ E♯ B♯

This is how the key signatures are written for sharp keys. Note the correct way to write a sharp symbol on a line or in a space:

Notice that each subsequent sharp is five letter names higher than the previous sharp, although the sharps are written in an alternately ascending and descending pattern, in order to fit the key signature on the staff. The interval between each sharp is a perfect 5th. Note there are various places on the staff where each sharp *could* be written. The above pattern is the one which is *conventionally* used, and it enables the musician to read key signatures at a glance.

Let's now look at flat key signatures. Flats also have a set order:

B♭ E♭ A♭ D♭ G♭ C♭ F♭

There are four letter names between each flat, and they occur at the interval of a perfect 4th. Note the correct way to write a flat on a line or in a space.

Various patterns have emerged concerning major keys and key signatures. Here is a summary of the rules:

The order of the sharp major keys

C G D A E B F♯ C♯
Each key is a perfect 5th higher (seven half steps) than the previous key.

The order of the sharps in the signature

F♯ C♯ G♯ D♯ A♯ E♯ B♯
Each sharp is a perfect 5th apart (seven half steps).

The order of the flat major keys

C F B♭ E♭ A♭ D♭ G♭ C♭
Each key is a perfect 4th higher (five half steps) than the previous key.

The order of flats in the signature

B♭ E♭ A♭ D♭ G♭ C♭ F♭
Each flat is a perfect 4th apart (five half steps).

Trace the pattern of key notes and the order of sharps and flats at the piano. It will help you to familiarize yourself with the distinctive qualities of a perfect 5th and a perfect 4th.

Enharmonic Keys

The term **enharmonic** can be translated as "sounding as one". It is used when a note changes its name, but *not* its pitch, for convenience in notation. We will now examine the use of the enharmonic concept in keys.

We have seen that there are fifteen key signatures. (There are no sharps or flats in C major). If you compare the key of B major (five sharps) with C♭ major (seven flats) at the keyboard, you will notice that both scales have exactly the same sound. The same may be said of the relationship between F♯ major (six sharps) and G♭ major (six flats), and also of the relationship between C♯ major (seven sharps) and D♭ major (five flats). Such pairs of keys represent alternate ways of writing the same sounds, and are called **enharmonic keys**.

To sum up, these are the three pairs of enharmonic major keys:

B major – C♭ major (5 sharps: 7 flats)

F♯ major – G♭ major (6 sharps: 6 flats)

C♯ major – D♭ major (7 sharps: 5 flats)

The uses of enharmonic keys will become clear after you have read the following section, which is concerned with the circular aspect of key relationships.

Key Circles

If you refer back to the section on tetrachords, you will observe that it is possible to create a link between flat major keys and the sharp major keys through C major.

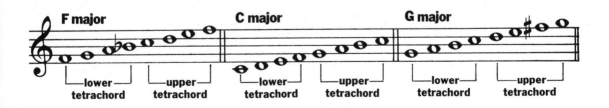

51

The above diagram implies that major flat keys and major sharp keys grow further away from each other in a linear pattern. If you study the **key circle** below, you will see that this is an erroneous image, and that the sounds within each key grow *towards* each other and link enharmonically at the base of the circle.

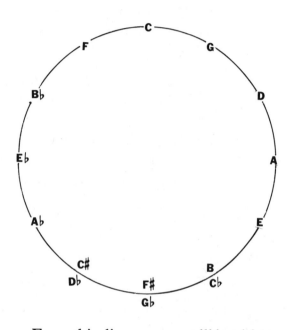

From this diagram, you will be able to work out how the enharmonic keys overlap. Enharmonic changes can be made from a sharp key to a flat key, or vice versa, while the piece is in progress, giving the composer access to the other side of the circle. The process of changing key is called **modulation**.

Double Sharps and Double Flats

You will remember that it is necessary in major scales to keep the letter names of notes in consecutive order. You may wonder whether such keys as G♯ major and F♭ major exist. They do on paper, but as both scales would involve the use of signs known as **double sharps** and **double flats** in order to keep the consecutive letter order, neither key is in common use. It is clearer to write G♯ major as A♭ major, and F♭ major as E major.

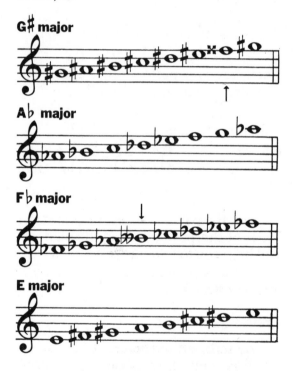

The notation must fulfil two requirements: the letter names must be consecutive, and intervals between the notes must conform to the step, step, half step, step, step, step, half step pattern. Thus, we discover the use for double sharps and double flats.

Double sharp   **Double flat**

A double sharp *raises* a note by two half steps, and a double flat *lowers* a note by two half steps. These signs are awkward to read, and keys which need them are avoided if possible.

Accidentals

There are two uses for this expression. First, a musician may use the term **accidental** to describe any note qualified by a sharp, double sharp, flat or double flat – i.e. any note that is not A B C D E F or G. Second, the term may be used to describe a note which is *foreign* to a given key. Thus, F♯ and C♯ belong to the key of D major, and would not be described as accidentals within the context of that key: but notes which do not belong to D major, such as E♭, F♮, A♭ and E♯ would be described as accidentals *within* that key. This is a more accurate usage.

There are five rules governing the use of accidentals which may be summarized as follows:

1. The sharp sign (♯) *raises* a natural "white" note by a half step, and the flat sign (♭) *lowers* a natural "white" note by a half step.

2. The double sharp sign (×) *raises* a natural "white" note by two half steps, and the double flat sign (♭♭) *lowers* a natural "white" note by two half steps.

3. The natural sign (♮) *cancels* a previous sharp (♯) or flat (♭). The natural sign can raise *or* lower a note.

4. The natural sign placed beside a sharp (♮♯) *lowers* a doubly sharpened note (×) by a half step. The natural sign placed beside a flat (♮♭) *raises* a doubly flattened note (♭♭) by a half step.

5. An accidental (a note foreign to the key) lasts only until the next barline unless previously cancelled. The barline acts as an automatic cancelling device.

53

Section C

The Structure of the Minor Scale

Minor keys create a totally different effect and feeling from major keys, and give the composer a completely contrasting set of tonal colors with which to create his music.

There are two forms of the minor scale. Both consist of eight notes ascending, and eight notes descending. Both forms have notes in common with the major scale beginning on the same key note, and also notes in common with each other. The two forms are called the **harmonic minor** and **melodic minor**. The harmonic minor scale rises and falls using the same notes and intervals throughout. The melodic minor scale is more complicated, as two patterns are contained within it. It uses one set of notes and intervals in its ascending pattern, and a slightly changed set of notes and intervals in its descending pattern.

Initially, try to grasp the similarities, and subsequently, the differences between the four patterns that have emerged: major, harmonic minor, ascending melodic minor, and descending melodic minor. The harmonic form is adopted by the composer in order to write harmony, but this form is unwieldy in the context of melody because the interval between the sixth and seventh degrees is awkward to sing – an important consideration in the composition of melody.

Let's now examine the similarities and differences contained within the harmonic and melodic forms of the minor scale. In the same way that our starting point in the major system was C major, so our starting point in the minor system will be A minor, because the key signature possesses no sharps or flats.

In *all* minor forms, the tonic, supertonic, mediant, sub-dominant and dominant remain the same. The changes take place *only* in the sub-mediant and leading note, and are marked by accidentals which do not appear in the key signature. Study the diagram below and look carefully at the sixth and seventh notes in each form.

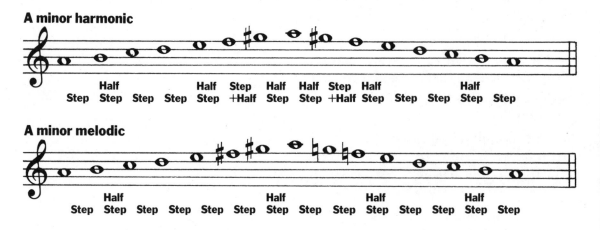

A minor harmonic

| Half | | | | Half | Step | Half | Half | Step | Half | | | Half | |
| Step | Step | Step | Step | Step | +Half | Step | Step | +Half | Step | Step | Step | Step | Step |

A minor melodic

| Half | | | | | | Half | | | Half | | | Half | |
| Step | Step | Step | Step | Step | Step | Step | Step | Step | Step | Step | Step | Step | Step |

Below is a summary of changes that occur in the sixth and seventh degrees of the scale of A minor.

Harmonic form

The seventh degree is *raised* by a half step from G to G♯ in the ascending and descending form. The sixth degree will correspond with the key signature.

Melodic ascending form

The sixth and seventh degrees are *both raised* by a half step: the sixth from F to F♯, and the seventh from G to G♯.

Melodic descending form

In this form, neither the sixth nor seventh degree is raised and thus they both correspond with the key signature.

The interval between the sixth and seventh degrees of the harmonic minor scale comprises three half steps, and is known as an **augmented 2nd**. In the context of a harmonic minor scale, it has an interesting and unusual sound, but it's awkward and unwieldy for the voice, and so is generally avoided in melody writing.

Play all forms of the scale of A minor on the piano. Listen very carefully to the sound of each form, especially above the dominant. Study the diagram below and memorize each interval.

A minor harmonic

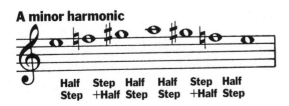

| Half Step | Step +Half | Half Step | Half Step | Step +Half | Half Step |

A minor melodic

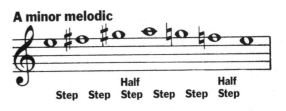

| | Step | Step | Half Step | Step | Step | Step | Half Step |

Comparison of Major and Minor Forms

First, compare the first five degrees of the major and minor forms, as this is the area of all minor scales which possesses a consistent set of intervals.

A major

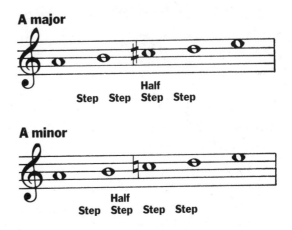

| | Step | Step | Half Step | Step |

A minor

| | Step | Half Step | Step | Step |

Note that the only difference occurs in the third degree: in the major scale, there is a step between the second and third degrees; in the minor scale there is only a half step. This is a consistent difference between *all* major and minor scales. One other useful comparison can be made – between the top four degrees of the major and minor forms.

A major

		Half	Half		
Step	Step	Step	Step	Step	Step

A minor harmonic

Half	Step	Half	Half	Step	Half
Step	+Half	Step	Step	+Half	Step

A minor melodic

		Half			Half
Step	Step	Step	Step	Step	Step

Notice that the interval between the seventh and eighth degrees is a half step in *all* ascending forms.

The information in this section is complicated. Try to establish a degree of familiarity with the material covered before attempting to adapt it to other keys, where there will be the additional complication of the sharps or flats in the key signature.

The Construction of Subsequent Sharp Minor Scales

The most important fact to remember is that every scale *must* conform to a given pattern. Tetrachords are not very useful in minor keys, because in each form of the minor scale the two tetrachords are different. Nevertheless, the four rules summarized at the end of the section on key signatures can be usefully applied here.

The first rule will help us to find the minor key with one sharp: the key note will be a perfect 5th above A. Thus, the minor key with one sharp in the key signature is E minor. In the diagram below you will see it written in the form that corresponds to the key signature:

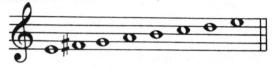

By raising the second degree of the scale by a half step from its natural form of F to F♯, one of the interval requirements of the scale is fulfilled: there must be a tone between the tonic and supertonic. Having established that the first five degrees of the scale will remain for all forms of the E minor scale, let's examine which of the top four degrees must be changed.

To transform the scale into the harmonic form, it is necessary to raise the seventh degree by a half step, creating D♯. This accidental will not appear in the key signature.

E minor harmonic

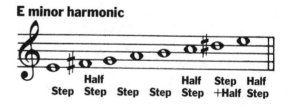

	Half			Half	Step	Half
Step	Step	Step	Step	Step	+Half	Step

To transform the scale into the ascending melodic form, it is necessary to raise the sixth degree by a half step, in addition to raising the seventh degree by a half step:

56

E minor melodic, ascending

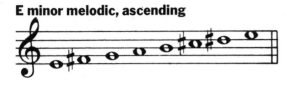

The descending melodic minor form corresponds to the form that fits the key signature:

E minor melodic, descending

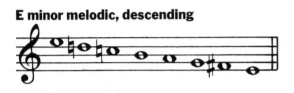

The minor key with two sharps begins on the note which is a perfect 5th above E. That key is B minor. The second

degree must be raised by a half step in order to conform to the pattern. This creates the new sharp – C♯. The pattern of sharps is the same for minor key signatures as for major key signatures. It is useful at this point to summarize the rules that have so far been established.

First, each subsequent sharp minor scale starts on the *fifth* degree of the previous scale.

Second, each scale will retain the sharps from the previous scale, and to those will be added the sharp that precedes the second degree of the scale.

In the diagram below are all the sharp minor scales, both harmonic and melodic, written without key signatures. Check the intervals of each one. (The half steps are marked with a bracket.)

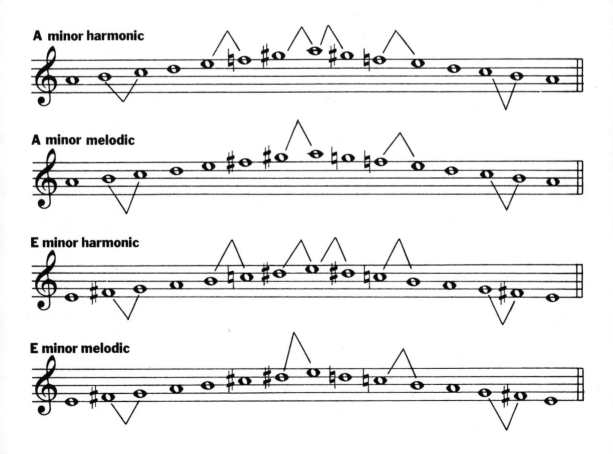

D♯ minor harmonic

D♯ minor melodic

A♯ minor harmonic

A♯ minor melodic

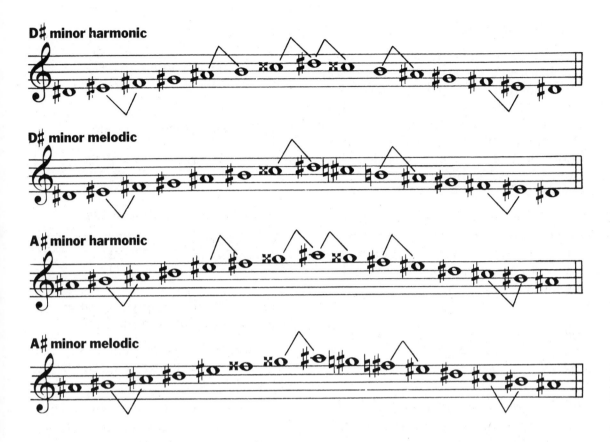

The key signatures applicable to minor keys modified by sharps are as follows:

A minor   **E minor**   **B minor**   **F♯ minor**

C♯ minor   **G♯ minor**   **D♯ minor**   **A♯ minor**

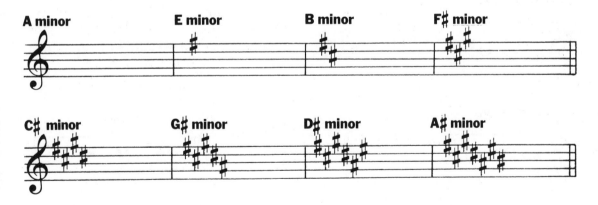

The order of sharps remains the same in both major and minor keys.

Flat Minor Scales

Refer back again to the four rules summarized at the end of the section on key signatures. To find the major key with one flat, we counted up five half steps (a perfect 4th) from C. To find the minor key with one flat we must count up five half steps (a perfect 4th) from A. Thus, the minor key with one flat is D Minor.

In flat minor keys, the sixth degree must be *lowered* by a half step in order to create the new accidental. This is the scale in correspondence with the key signature:

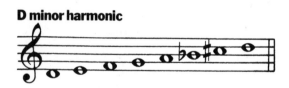

The scale is transformed into the harmonic form by raising the seventh degree by a half step:

D minor harmonic

Here is the scale transformed into the melodic ascending and descending forms by raising and lowering the sixth and seventh degrees by a half step:

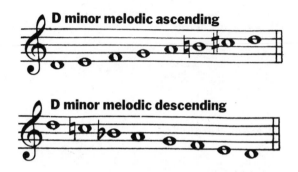

The rules that apply to flat minor scales may be thus summarized:

First, each subsequent flat minor scale begins on the fourth degree of the previous scale.

Second, each scale will retain the flats from the previous scale and to those will be added the flat that precedes the sixth degree of the scale.

In the diagram below are all the flat minor scales, both harmonic and melodic, written without key signatures. Check the intervals of each one.

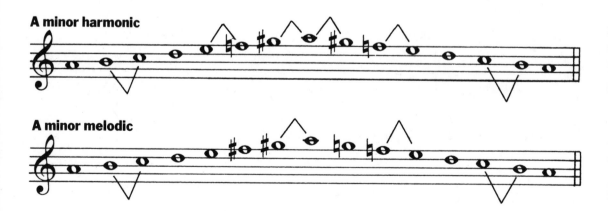

D minor harmonic

D minor melodic

G minor harmonic

G minor melodic

C minor harmonic

C minor melodic

F minor harmonic

F minor melodic

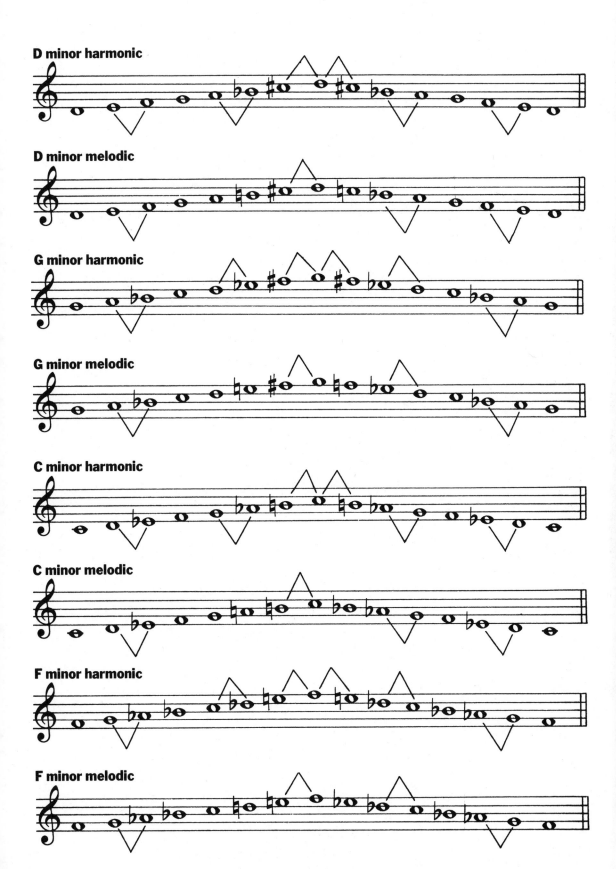

B♭ minor harmonic

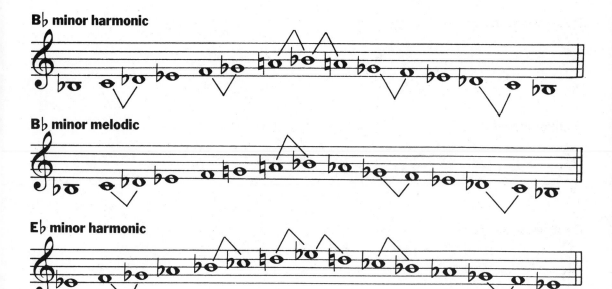

B♭ minor melodic

E♭ minor harmonic

E♭ minor melodic

A♭ minor harmonic

A♭ minor melodic

The key signatures applicable to minor keys modified by flats are as follows:

The order of flats remains the same in both major and minor keys.

The Minor Key Circle

As in the major key circle, the flat keys are on the left side of the circle. The enharmonic keys appear at the base.

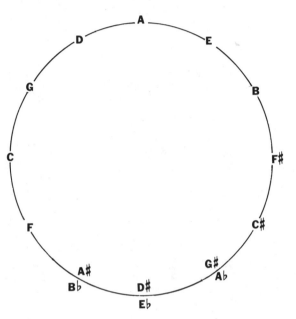

These are the enharmonic minor keys:

G♯ Minor – A♭ Minor (5 sharps: 7 flats)

D♯ Minor – E♭ Minor (6 sharps: 6 flats)

A♯ Minor – B♭ Minor (7 sharps: 5 flats)

The Intervals of the Minor Scale

The chart below analyses and compares each interval in the different forms of the A minor scale – harmonic, melodic ascending, and melodic descending.

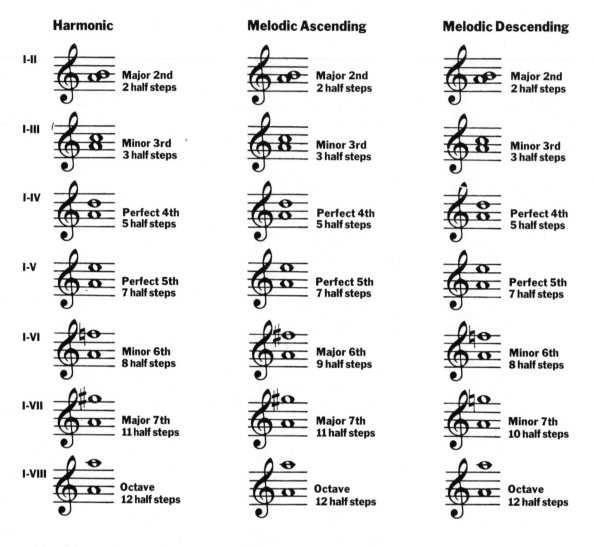

	Harmonic	Melodic Ascending	Melodic Descending
I-II	Major 2nd / 2 half steps	Major 2nd / 2 half steps	Major 2nd / 2 half steps
I-III	Minor 3rd / 3 half steps	Minor 3rd / 3 half steps	Minor 3rd / 3 half steps
I-IV	Perfect 4th / 5 half steps	Perfect 4th / 5 half steps	Perfect 4th / 5 half steps
I-V	Perfect 5th / 7 half steps	Perfect 5th / 7 half steps	Perfect 5th / 7 half steps
I-VI	Minor 6th / 8 half steps	Major 6th / 9 half steps	Minor 6th / 8 half steps
I-VII	Major 7th / 11 half steps	Major 7th / 11 half steps	Minor 7th / 10 half steps
I-VIII	Octave / 12 half steps	Octave / 12 half steps	Octave / 12 half steps

In this context the word "major" means "greater" and the word "minor" means "smaller." It does *not* mean that major intervals occur only in major keys, or that minor intervals occur only in minor keys.

Relative Keys

Because key signatures for major and minor keys are the same, it is not possible to tell at a glance which key is intended. The melody will often provide clues. Many melodies begin and end on the tonic. Sometimes, in minor keys, accidentals will provide some help because they are likely to concern the sixth and seventh degrees of the scale. Major and minor keys which possess the same *key signature* are called **relative keys.** The following pairs are relative keys.

SHARPS

C major – A minor

G major – E minor

D major – B minor

A major – F♯ minor

E major – C♯ minor

B major – G♯ minor

F♯ major – D♯ minor

C♯ major – A♯ minor

FLATS

C major – A minor

F major – D minor

B♭ major – G minor

E♭ major – C minor

A♭ major – F minor

D♭ major – B♭ minor

G♭ major – E♭ minor

C♭ major – A♭ minor

Major and minor keys which share the same *tonic* are said to be **parallel keys.**

Below is an example of a melody in a minor key – the beginning of the 1st movement of Symphony No. 40 in G minor by Mozart. Observe the use of the harmonic minor accidentals:

SECTION D

The Chromatic Scale

The word "chromatic" means colorful. A **chromatic scale** is the collection of all twelve half steps that fill each octave. A chromatic scale may start on any note and then ascend or descend through twelve consecutive half steps until the tonic, one octave above or below, is reached. The harmonic chromatic scale is written in such a way that each note can be harmonized in relation to the tonic of that scale.

Let us take C chromatic scale as our example. First of all, write all the notes of the scale of C major. Then add to them the notes in both forms of C minor that do not occur in the major scale:

Only two more notes now need to be added to complete the chromatic scale of C. The first note is between C and D; the second between F and G. Should the first be C♯ or D♭ and the second F♯ or G♭? The answers are D♭ and F♯. These notes are needed in the formation of some of the harmony associated with the key of C major. D♭ is a diatonic half step above the tonic, and F♯ is a diatonic half step below the dominant. A **diatonic half step** is one where the two notes that comprise the half step have *different* letter names. If the two notes have the *same* letter name, it is then called a **chromatic half step.** Here is the complete scale:

The Intervals of the Chromatic Scale

This will complete your vocabulary of common intervals that occur within the span of an octave. The intervals which sound the same are bracketed together. Each would be used in a different harmonic context.

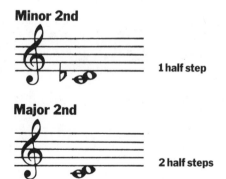

Minor 2nd
1 half step

Major 2nd
2 half steps

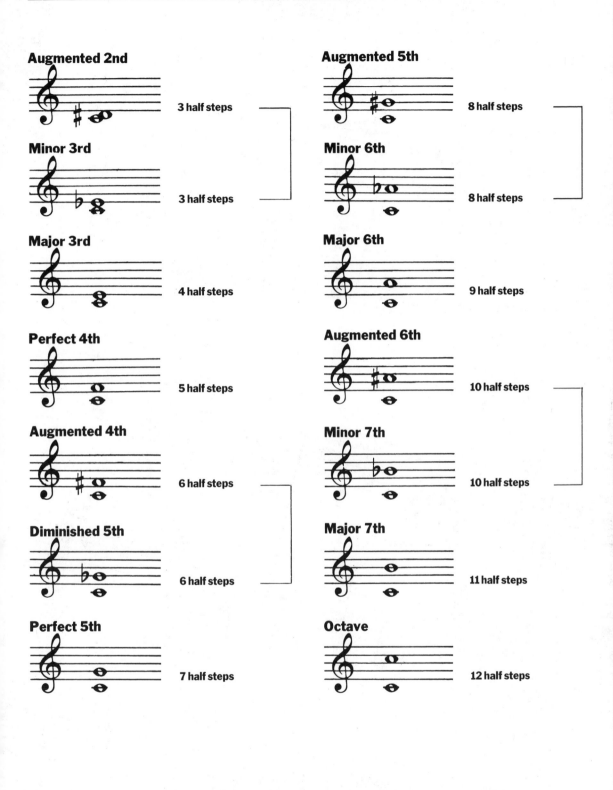

Augmented 2nd

3 half steps

Minor 3rd

3 half steps

Major 3rd

4 half steps

Perfect 4th

5 half steps

Augmented 4th

6 half steps

Diminished 5th

6 half steps

Perfect 5th

7 half steps

Augmented 5th

8 half steps

Minor 6th

8 half steps

Major 6th

9 half steps

Augmented 6th

10 half steps

Minor 7th

10 half steps

Major 7th

11 half steps

Octave

12 half steps

4

TRANSPOSITION
AND SCORE READING

Transposition

To **transpose** is to re-write a given piece, or section of a piece, in a key which is different from that of the original. It is not a difficult task if the student possesses a sound knowledge of intervals. Look at the example below and follow through the method for transposing the melody into B major.

First, establish the key of the melody: it is G major. The next task is to write the key signature of B major on a fresh staff (F♯ C♯ G♯ D♯ A♯) followed by the time signature. Establish the interval between the two key notes, G–B: it is a major third (four half steps). Thus, each note in the melody must be raised by a major 3rd, giving the following result:

The first three notes of the melody are the first, third and fifth degrees of the scale of G major. When the melody is transposed into B major, the first three notes will be the first, third and fifth degrees of the scale of B major. This is a way to check the accuracy of your transposition.

Accidentals will *not* necessarily remain the same in the new key. The interval must be calculated very carefully where an accidental is involved. Below you will see an example of transposition where the accidentals are changed in order to keep the intervals consistent.

Beethoven

The passage is in A minor. Below it is transposed down a major 3rd to F minor:

Let us now examine one of the uses of transposition. Sometimes it may be necessary for a pianist, when accompanying a singer, to transpose a melody into a lower or higher key, so that it will be appropriate for their specific vocal range. A skilled musician possessing a good aural sense can transpose a piece into a different key at sight, without needing to write it out in the new key. Sometimes it may be necessary to transpose music up or down an octave, and this will usually involve a change of clef, though not a change of key.

Transposing Instruments

Certain musical instruments sound at a pitch which is different from the written pitch. This process is incorporated in the mechanism of the instrument, and requires no conscious effort on the part of the player. Imagine that a piano has been deliberately tuned a step lower than is normal, so that every note sounds a step lower than would be expected. If the tune below **(a)** which is in C major, were played on a piano tuned a step below normal pitch, it would sound in B♭ major, as in **(b)**:

If we were obliged to use this hypothetical piano with other instruments which were tuned to normal pitch, it would be necessary to make an adjustment to the notation of the music written for the piano. The music for this instrument would be written in D major – as in **(c)** – in order that the actual sounds produced should sound in C major, as in **(a)**:

There are many transposing orchestral instruments. These instruments can be played more easily when the notation is transposed, because the player will have the least number of sharps and flats to negotiate.

This system helps the player, but can cause difficulties for students of score-reading. For there may be ten or more different transpositions in a large orchestral score. This method of score writing has never been seriously challenged because, in an orchestral context, it makes the rehearsal process simpler if both player and conductor work from the same notation. If the transposed parts were written at pitch in the full score, the conductor would need to transpose when indicating errors, or making interpretive suggestions to the player. It is generally considered to be simpler to provide the conductor with transposed notation. Most students would consider this to be a matter worthy of debate.

Transposition is obviously an important skill, but at this stage it is more important to understand how the system works, and how to take it into consideration when reading the notation used by a **transposing instrument**, than to be able to apply the skill to your own instrument.

The Transposing Instruments of the Orchestra

These are the most frequently found transpositions in an orchestral score:

Instruments in A

Clarinet Cornet Trumpet	**These sound a minor 3rd lower than written pitch.**

Instruments in Bb

Clarinet Trumpet Cornet Soprano Saxophone	**These sound a major 2nd (a step) lower than written pitch.**
Bass Clarinet Tenor Saxophone	**These sound one octave plus a step lower than written pitch.**

Instruments in D

Trumpet Clarinet	**These sound a major 2nd (a step) higher than written pitch.**

Instruments in Eb

Clarinet	**This sounds a minor 3rd higher than written pitch.**
Alto Clarinet Alto Saxophone	**These sound a major 6th lower than written pitch.**
Baritone Saxophone	**This sounds an octave plus a major 6th lower than written pitch.**

Instruments in F

Trumpet	**This sounds a perfect 4th higher than written pitch.**
Bassett Horn French Horn English Horn	**These sound a perfect 5th lower than written pitch.**

Instruments that transpose either up or down the octave are not considered to be true transposing instruments, as the transposition they make is merely one of pitch, not one of key. Instruments in this category are the piccolo, which sounds an octave higher than the written pitch, and the double-bass and contra-bassoon which sound an octave lower than written pitch. The guitar also sounds an octave lower than written pitch.

Below you will see two sections of the full score of an orchestral piece by Smetana called "Vltava", one of a set of tone poems known collectively as *Má Vlast (My Fatherland)*. Smetana lived from 1824 to 1884, and was a native of the country we now know as Czechoslovakia. "Vltava" is written for a large orchestra and strongly reflects Smetana's interest in the traditional music of Bohemia.

In the first example, notice that the instruments are grouped according to type, and that within each group, the higher pitched instruments are placed at the top. The instrumental groups appear in the following order: first the woodwind, followed by the brass, the percussion, the harp, and lastly, the strings. In order to find out which instruments are used in an orchestral piece, look at the first page of the score, where you will see all the instruments listed. If there is a solo instrument or voice, it will appear immediately above the strings.

Die Moldau‑Vltava

Bedřich Smetana
(1824-1884)

Allegro(a 2 batt) commodo non agitato

Die erste Quelle der Moldau (První pramen Vltavy)

This second extract is known as a **"tutti"** passage, indicating that the whole orchestra is playing together.

Die Moldau strömt breit dahin (Široký tok Vltavy)

5
GLOSSARY OF TERMS

Glossary of Terms

This is a glossary of terms and signs commonly used in music to give the performer some indication of the manner in which a piece is to be played. Terms are traditionally expressed in the Italian language, but occasionally French and German are used. As this glossary includes only the most common terms, they are exclusively Italian.

The terms fall into six main groups:

1. The **tempo,** or speed, at which the music is to be played.

2. The dynamic level at which the music is to be played. **Dynamics** are concerned with the degree of loudness, or softness, of the music.

3. The mood, feeling, or style of the music.

4. A group of terms referring to general instructions which cannot be categorized under any specific heading.

5. The **articulation** and **phrasing** of the music.

6. Signs appearing on the staff.

1. Tempo

(a) Indications of a stable speed

Lento – Very slow

Largo – Very slow, broad

Larghetto – Rather slow, but not as slow as *Largo*

Adagio – Slow

Grave – Slow, solemn

Andante – At walking speed

Moderato – Moderate speed

Andantino – Slightly faster than *Andante*

Allegretto – Moderately fast, but not as fast as *allegro*

Allegro – Fast and lively

Vivace – Lively

Presto – Very fast

Prestissimo – Very, very fast

Giusto – In exact time

Tempo commodo – At a convenient speed

L'istesso tempo – The speed of the beat remains the same, although the notation changes.

(b) Indications of a change in the speed

Abbreviations are shown in brackets.

Accelerando (Accel.) – Gradually faster

Allargando (Allarg.) – Getting slower, probably with a broader sound

A tempo – Resuming normal speed after a deviation

Calando – Decreasing both speed and dynamic level

Doppio movimento – Twice as fast; at double speed

Meno mosso – Less movement, immediately slower

Più allegro – Faster

Più mosso – More movement; immediately faster

Più moto – Immediately faster

Rallentando (Rall.) – Becoming gradually slower

Ritardando (Ritard.) – Gradually slower

Ritenuto (Rit.) – Held back

Slentando – Gradually slower

Stringendo (String.) Gradually faster

Tempo primo – Resume the original speed

2. Dynamics

(a) Indications of a stable dynamic level

Pianissimo (pp) – Very soft

Piano (p) – Soft

Mezzo piano (mp) – Moderately soft

Mezzo forte (mf) – Moderately loud

Forte (f) – Loud

Fortissimo (ff) – Very loud

(b) Indications of a change in the dynamic level

Calando – Decreasing both speed and dynamic level

Crescendo (Cresc.) – Becoming gradually louder

Decrescendo (Decresc.) – Becoming gradually softer

Diminuendo (Dim.) – Becoming gradually softer

Forte piano (fp) – Loud, then soft

Morendo – Dying away

Perdendosi – Dying away (and becoming gradually slower)

Più forte – Louder

Più piano – Softer

Sforzando (sf) – A strong accent

Smorzando (Smorz.) – Dying away

3. Mood, feeling and style

A cappela – In a church style: unaccompanied choral music

Ad libitum (Ad lib.) – At will; the speed and style are left to the performer

A piacere – At will; at the pleasure of the performer

Affrettando – Hurrying

Agitato – Agitated

Alla marcia – In the style of a march

Animato – Animated

Appassionato – With passion

Bravura – Boldness and spirit

Brillante – Brilliantly

Cantabile – In a singing style

Cantando – In a singing style

Con amore – With love and tenderness

Con anima – With deep feeling, with soul

Con brio – With vigour

Con forza – With force

Con fuoco – With fire

Con grazia – With grace

Con moto – With movement

Con spirito – With spirit

Deciso – Decisively

Delicato – Delicately

Dolce – Sweetly

Dolcissimo – Very gently, sweetly

Dolente – Sadly

Dolore – Grief or sorrow

Doloroso – With sorrow

Energico – With energy

Espressione – Expression

Espressivo (Espress.) – With expression

Facile – Easy

Furioso – Furiously

Giocoso – With humour

Glissando (Gliss.) – To slide through a series of adjacent notes.

Impetuoso – Impetuously

Lacrimoso – Sadly

Largamente – Broadly

Legato – Smoothly

Leggiero – Light, delicate

Lontano – As from a distance

Lusingando – In a coaxing style, soothingly

Maestoso – Grandly, majestically

Marcato – In a marked style – with an emphasis on each note

Marziale – Martial

Mesto – Sadly

Mezza voce – In a half voice

Misterioso – Mysteriously

Nobilmente – Noble

Parlando – In a speaking style

Pastorale – In a pastoral style

Pesante – Heavily

Piacevole – Agreeable

Piangevole – Plaintively

Pomposo – Very dignified, pompously

Precipitoso – Impetuously

Rigoroso – Strictly

Risoluto – Resolute, bold

Rubato – "Robbed time" – in a flexible, expressive style

Scherzando – Playful

Semplice – Simply

Serioso – In a serious style

Soave – Gentle, smooth, sweet

Sonore – Sonorous

Sostenuto – Sustained

Sotto voce – In an undertone

Spiritoso – Spirited

Staccato – Detached

Strepitoso – Noisy, boisterous

Tranquillo – Tranquil, calm

Vigoroso – Boldly, with vigour

Vivo – In a lively style

Volante – Flying; swift and light

4. General Terms

A – At, to, by, for, in

Arco – With the bow (in string music)

Assai – Very

Ben – Well

Con – With

Da Capo (D.C.) – From the beginning

Dal Segno (D.S.) – From the sign 𝄋

Fine – The end

Ma – But

Meno – Less

Molto – Much

Non – Not

Pausa – Pause, or rest

Poco a poco – Little by little

Più – More

Pizzicato (pizz.) – Plucked (in string music)

Quasi – As if, almost

Segue – Follow at once

Sempre – Always

Senza – Without

Simile – In a like manner

Subito – Suddenly

Tacet – Be silent

Tenuto – Held

Troppo – Too much

Tutti – All

Un poco – A little

5. Articulation

There are many signs and terms which indicate how notes should be articulated, either separated from each other or joined smoothly together.

A **tie** is a curved line which joins two or more notes of *identical* pitch, creating a continuous sound.

A **slur** is a curved line which joins two or more notes of *differing* pitch. They should be played or sung smoothly.

A **phrase mark**

demonstrates the composer's indication of natural punctuation within the music. There is no set rule for phrase length, and often the use of different phrase lengths adds interest in the melody. The end of a phrase may provide the singer or wind player with an opportunity to take breath; but this is a secondary consideration – the shape and nuance of the melody come first.

Staccato is expressed by a dot over or under the note, and indicates that the note should be shortened, thus detaching it from the next note.

Accent These signs indicate that the note should be played with a strong stress or accent applied at the beginning of the note. The following terms also indicate an accent:

Sforzando (*sf* or *sz*) – a strong accent

Rinforzando (*rf*) – a reinforcement

Legato is the term which indicates that a group of notes should be played smoothly.

6. Signs on the Staff

| Clef | Key signature | Time Signature | Barline | Double barline |

| Repeat sign | Rest | Pause | Slur | Tie |

Crescendo (cresc.) Decrescendo (decresc.) / Diminuendo (dim.)

Becoming gradually louder   Becoming gradually softer

The octave sign – **8**ve, **8**va or **8,** – when shown above the staff, indicates that the passage must be played or sung an octave higher:

O The Grand Old Duke of York

written sound   actual sound

When this sign appears below the staff, it indicates that the passage must be played or sung an octave lower:

My Bonnie Lies Over The Ocean

written sound   actual sound